# CONTENTS

# Welcome
## Ceud Mile Failte

(A hundred thousand welcomes)

*I extend the famous Gaelic welcome to our visitors and hope that they will have a memorable and happy visit to our family home. I was brought up and educated here from the age of five and, as an only child, was lucky enough to inherit Ballindalloch from my late father, Sir Ewan Macpherson-Grant, 6th Baronet of Ballindalloch.*

In 1967 I had travelled 'o'er the border' to London and married Oliver Russell. We returned to live at Ballindalloch Castle in 1978 and have been tackling the challenge of modernising a traditional Highland Estate ever since. Having the diversified mixture of activities with the Castle as the central focus makes the Estate viable, and the family home secure for future generations.

Our visitors have always remarked on the homely and friendly atmosphere at Ballindalloch, and appreciated our high standard of maintenance. This is very much the memory we wish visitors to take away with them. Our family and all the staff who work here will then feel that our guardianship of the Castle has been worthwhile.

## Haste ye back!

*Clan Macpherson. Grant Russell*
*Laird of Ballindalloch.*

# BALLINDALLOCH CASTLE

*is first and foremost the much loved family home of the Macpherson-Grants. It is one of the very few privately owned Castles to have been lived in continuously by its original family. Ballindalloch is one of Scotland's most romantic castles, set in the magnificent surroundings of the Spey Valley and known as 'The Pearl of the North'.*

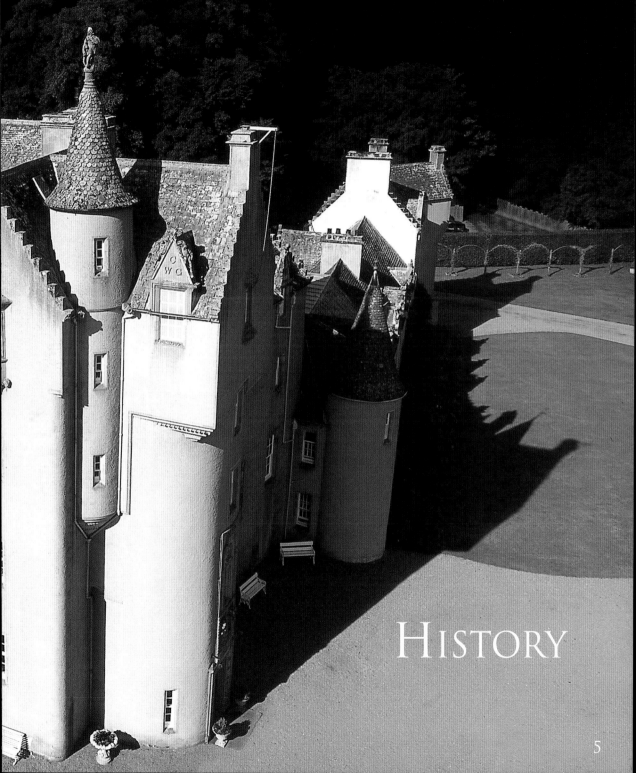

# HISTORY

TOUCH NOT THE CAT BOT A GLOVE

6

*On historical and stylistic grounds the old tower clearly dates from the early 16th century. The exact year of its origin is unknown, but the date 1546 is carved on a stone lintel in one of the bedrooms.*

The Castle was originally built on the traditional Z plan but subsequently has been greatly altered and enlarged. An interesting and unusual feature is the original front entrance, to the west of the Castle, opening into a circular stone staircase winding up to the cap-house or 'Watch Tower' dated 1602. There is a belief that the Castle was originally started on a hill above its present location. The foundations are still to be seen and legend has it that the then Laird of Ballindalloch started building there, but was compelled to change the site when every night the building was blown to the ground by some invisible agent. A voice was heard to repeat '*Build it in the coo-haugh*' and so that is where the Castle stands today.

*Ballindalloch Castle exemplifies the transition from the stark tower house necessary in 16th century Scotland to the elegant and comfortable country house so beloved of the Victorians in the Highlands.*

In 1770, General Grant added two new wings: one wing to the south where the Drawing Room is situated and one wing to the north. General Grant was one of the most noted *Bon Viveurs* of his day and the north wing was added specifically to house his favourite French chef. When travelling he was always accompanied by his cooks and it was his established custom 'not to hazard his palate on any dish until its quality had been previously ascertained'. Apart from his gastronomic interests he had a very successful military and political career, fighting in the American Wars of Independence and becoming Governor of East Florida in 1763. His unique personality added a lively and interesting component to the life of the countries where he lived.

He was succeeded by his grand-nephew George Macpherson of Invereshie who in 1838 was created a Baronet as Sir George Macpherson-Grant, 1st Baronet of Ballindalloch. In his name he symbolically united the two great clans of Strathspey.

The most extensive alterations and renovations (designed by Thomas MacKenzie) were carried out by Sir John Macpherson-Grant

(2nd Baronet) in 1850. The major addition was the building of the courtyard and the surrounding wings.

Sir George Macpherson-Grant (3rd Baronet) felt the Castle was a trifle small and added yet another nine rooms in 1878. He is remembered for his work in founding the famous Ballindalloch herd of Aberdeen-Angus cattle in 1860. It is now the oldest herd in the world.

In 1965 a major reconstruction was carried out by Sir Ewan Macpherson-Grant (6th Baronet). The main alteration was the demolition of the most recent wing of 1878, much to the improvement of the appearance of the building. At the same time the opportunity was taken to modernise and restore the Castle, adding five bathrooms to the previous total of one!

In 1978, the present Laird of Ballindalloch and her husband Oliver Russell moved into the Castle with their children: Guy, Edward and Lucy. Each year the family continue to renovate the castle inside and out.

THE PRESENT LAIRD OF BALLINDALLOCH AND HER FAMILY ~
An oil painting in the Dining Room by Paco Carvajal

*Catalogue of Books*
*Belonging to*
*Major William Grant of*

*Ballindalloch*

*Novr 11th 1766*

# A Tour of the Castle

# THE HALL

*With its grand staircase and its most unusual umbrella design and delightful fan vaulting, the Hall was designed by Thomas MacKenzie as part of the 1850 renovation.*

Over the fireplace are a number of fine 18th century pistols. The brass bevelled ones were used for sea service. Also of naval interest, though more modern - and to bring some of Russell influence into the 'Grant domain' is the naval dress sword of Admiral The Hon. Sir Guy Russell, Mr Russell's father who was 2nd Sea Lord and Principal ADC to the Queen in 1953-55. The Scottish dirks were used for hunting or dispatching enemies, but never draw a dirk unless to kill, for the legend goes '*Draw me not in anger Nor sheath me in dishonour*'.

Of interest is the china in the Sheraton corner cupboard (obscured by the pillar in the photograph opposite) by Ridgeway circa 1820. Also note the fine 'Bureau Plat' of the Louis Quinze period and the set of Scottish chairs made in Chippendale style with unusual carvings of bells. The commode is an example of fine English Marquetry and the bureau an example of rather bolder Dutch Marquetry.

# DRAWING ROOM

*Commissioned in 1770 by General James Grant, this portrait of him as a young boy in military uniform is the work of Richard Waitt, an early 18th century Scottish artist who specialised in painting members of the Grant family.*

Another painting of the distinguished General and Governor of Florida, as a rather older man, can be seen in the Dining Room upstairs.

The cut glass chandelier with its ormolu border of English roses and Scottish thistles is from the 18th century- possibly designed to celebrate the Union in 1707.

*A caricature of General James Grant in 1798*

Most of the furniture is 18th century
but of particular note are the pair of
card tables on either side of the
fireplace, the oval Sheraton work table
and the beautiful gilt mirror (circa
1755). The majority of the china is
German (18th and 19th century) with
the exception of the collection of early
Victorian Coalbrookdale (circa 1840).

The family portraits are all by Richard
Waitt, an early 18th-century Scottish
artist, who specialised in painting
members of the Grant family.

Either side of the fireplace are pictures
of King Philip V of Spain and Queen
Maria Louisa of Spain by Michael
Melendez (1679 - 1731).

*Above the fireplace is the Laird's favourite
painting of 'Peasants in an Inn', painted on
wood by David Teniers the Younger.*

# SMOKING ROOM

*Off the Drawing Room is the Laird's Smoking Room. After dinner the air would be rich with tales of hill and loch, when the Laird and his gentlemen friends would sit down to enjoy a dram or two.*

One window display houses some Chinese porcelain of the Qian Long period. The most important pieces are the bough pots which were designed in 1770 for the Parisian market but were never exported. The other is filled with German china from between 1770 and 1900 including Meissen and Dresden.

*One of a pair of 18th century 'pot pourri' containers bought by the present Lady Laird of Ballindalloch some years ago for £5. Much to her surprise a major antique house has now added a few noughts to their value!*

# LIBRARY

*The Library was redesigned and panelled in 1850 as part of the remodelling by Sir John Macpherson-Grant.*

The Library was redesigned and panelled in 1850 as part of the remodelling by Sir John Macpherson-Grant. In here there are 2,500 volumes, and the collection is said to be one of the best country house libraries in Scotland. Having avoided any major dispersal, it provides a three dimensional history of the cultural, literary and artistic development of the family.

The two main collectors were Colonel William Grant, in the early half of the 18th century, and Sir John Macpherson-Grant a century later. The Colonel collected most of the English Classics and French books, and Sir John acquired all the Spanish books while he was secretary to the Legation in Lisbon in 1850.

*While in Iberia, Sir John also collected the many fine Spanish paintings hung in the Castle. These pictures are acknowledged to be the most important private collection of 17th century Spanish paintings in Scotland and one of the earliest to have been brought from Spain.*

*St Ursula*
*by Jusepe de Ribera*

*St James in Tomb*
*by Francisco Ribalta*

*This wing of the house was built
during the 18th century by
General James Grant.*

The magnificent four-poster bed (circa 1860) is
Scottish, made in cherry-wood, and most of the other
furniture is 18th century. The delightful Macpherson-
Grant family portraits were painted by Crispini in 1864.

The beautiful ladies dressing case (circa 1870) was
found by the Laird in one of the attics. It was still
wrapped in its original brown paper and string. It was
probably an unopened wedding present - somebody is
still waiting for a thank you note!

# DINING ROOM

*This is the largest room in the Castle and was originally the Great Hall of the 16th century Castle.*

During that period the appearance of the room would have been rather different. At one end would have been a raised dais or platform on which the laird and his 'leddy' would have sat at a high table while lesser mortals, those 'below the salt', would have sat at one long table stretching the length of the room.

In place of today's Persian carpet the stone-flagged floor would have been covered with fresh rushes, gathered every day from the meadows of the coohaugh around the Castle. The windows would have been rather smaller in the interests of defence, and would also have been protected by iron bars. In place of today's fine panelling the rough stone walls might have been adorned with tapestries showing the Pleasures of the Chase or legendary incidents in the history of the clan.

It was in this room, according to Sir Thomas Dick Lauder, that one of the early Grants of Ballindalloch hospitably entertained the neighbouring Laird of Tullochcarron, whose nearby castle was much too close for comfort. The best Glenlivet was much in evidence and the unsuspecting Tullochcarron drank not wisely but too well. Suddenly at an appointed signal from the Laird of Ballindalloch, all his henchmen drew their dirks and brandished them at Tullochcarron. However, the story has a happy ending. Mindful of the dirks and the dungeon below, Tullochcarron was only too willing to sign the papers which were flourished at him and, while he was allowed to escape with his life, his lands have ever afterwards been carefully looked after as part of the Ballindalloch Estate.

As part of the 1850 alterations, the room was redesigned and panelled in American pine; the design of the ceiling was derived from casts taken from Craigievar Castle, Aberdeenshire. The magnificent fireplace with the coats of arms of the Macphersons and the Grants was also erected then. 'Ense et Animo' is the Grant family motto; 'Touch not the Cat Bot a Glove' is the Macpherson one - in other words 'Don't meddle with a Macpherson without a glove on'!

Visitors might be lucky enough to see 'The Green Lady' in the Dining Room, where she is said to appear from time to time.

*Most of the silver cups were won by Sir George Macpherson-Grant, 3rd Baronet, for his world-famous prize-winning Aberdeen Angus cattle.*

The paintings of George III and Queen Charlotte, by Allan Ramsay, were presented to General James Grant in recognition of his military services in the American Wars of Independence.

*In the corridor leading to the Nursery are one or two treasured pictures of the castle by the Laird when a child*

# NURSERY

*The Nursery represents a history of 'young lairds & lassies' from the late 18th century until modern times.*

From the beautiful inlaid Georgian high-chair (circa 1770) to the cane and mahogany cradle (circa 1830) the much loved 19th and 20th century teddies and the modern dolls' house (1975) made by Mr Oliver Russell for his daughter Lucy, the Castle's Nursery has something for all children - or simply those young at heart!

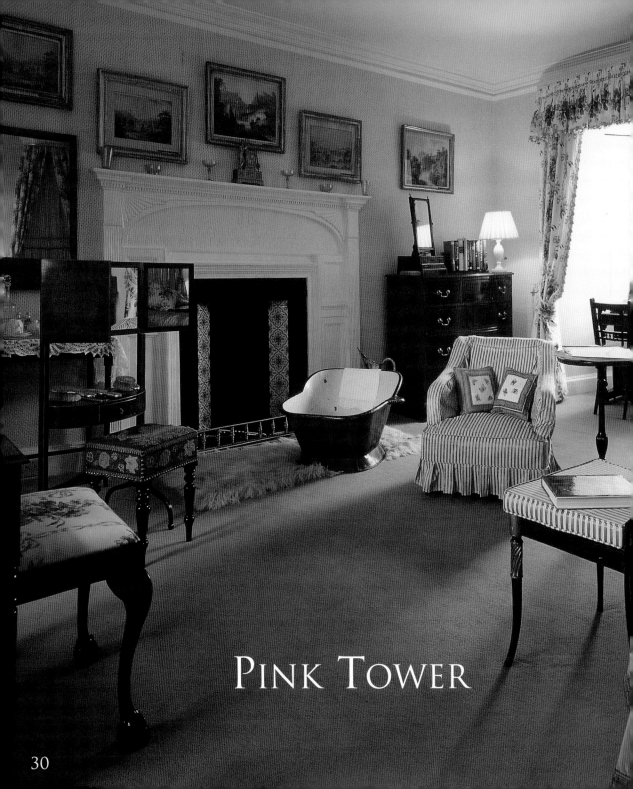

PINK TOWER

*This is one of the original bedrooms in the Castle as you can see from the stone lintel over the mantelpiece commemorating the marriage of John Grant and Barbara Gordon in 1546.*

The beautiful lady (a vision in pink) reclining in the armchair is said to be the present Laird of Ballindalloch's guardian angel. She was a Macpherson-Grant relation who lost a child of five years old in 1750 and when the Laird came to live here, also as a child of five, the lady thought that she was her long lost child. Unknown to the Laird, she has nearly died three times in her life and three times the lady, her guardian angel, has saved her.

# HIGHLAND TOWER

*The handsome circular stair tower, circa 1546 (which changes direction halfway and rises to the Watch tower) reveals the true antiquity of the Castle.*

It is interesting to note the amazing width of the walls which rise to over 100ft - no cranes in those days, just manpower! You will notice in the walls 'Crosslet loopholes' (now covered in harling) where the Macpherson-Grant henchmen used to sit with their arrows and hagbuts, waiting for enemies to approach within range. On ascending you will pass the servants' bedrooms and original 16th century privy. Then on upwards to the Watch tower from where they guarded the Castle. You will also see the Corbelled Machicolation which was a cunning 16th century device from which they used to throw stones and sewage onto the heads of unwanted visitors at the front door!

34

*Glen Feshie by*
*William Beattie Brown*

GOD'S GARDEN.

THE KISS OF THE SUN FOR PARDON
THE SONG OF THE BIRDS FOR MIRTH.
ONE IS NEARER GOD'S HEART IN A GARDEN.
THAN ANYWHERE ELSE ON EARTH.

*The Ballindalloch Rose*

# THE GARDENS
## AN UNFORGETTABLE ENCOUNTER

*Ballindalloch Castle Gardens, set in the glorious Scottish Highlands, are a must for every visitor to the area.*

This fairytale Castle has magnificent grounds which will hold the visitor spellbound with their beauty. From the lovely 'Ballindalloch Rose' to the majestic tree-lined walks, this surely must be the most memorable part of any outing. From the Castle's opening in Spring, through to its closure in the Autumn, the Gardens remain spectacular.

*The Laird, a dog lover, has made sure that the Ballindalloch Gardens cater for any visiting pooch by setting aside a special dog-walking area.*

The Ballindalloch Doocot dated 1696 has 844 stone nesting boxes. In Scotland, pigeons are known as doos and every castle had its doocot, for the doos fed themselves at the expense of neighbouring farmers and were a source of fresh meat during hard winters. Besides their culinary value, doos had medicinal properties; warm pigeon hearts were applied to the feet to cure a fever. Further, doo dung was supposed to be a wonderful cure for baldness - perhaps a justified belief following recent evidence that those working on intensive chicken farms become more hirsute!

# BALLINDALLOCH CASTLE GOLF COURSE

*This magnificent Championship standard golf course was designed by Donald Steel and Tom Mackenzie, both internationally recognised golf course architects with courses in over fifteen countries.*

They created a heady mix of challenging golf and aesthetic appeal, just as they have done at their other famous Scottish design, the Carnegie course at Skibo Castle. With its nine holes and eighteen tees, the course provides a fair test for golfers of all standards and is well placed to become known as the finest nine-hole course in Scotland. The course is set on the banks of the River Avon, among 150 year old trees and with marvellous views of the surrounding purple heather-clad hills and native birch woods.

*'Ballindalloch Golf Course is the perfect place to find escape from an imperfect world. By the imaginative use of alternative tees, it has achieved the illusion of making nine holes into 18. Purists who scoff at the idea would be missing a treat if they passed it by. For natural beauty and golf played to the tune of wind and river it is worth seeking out. Such days should never end.'*

*Parkinson on Monday - The Daily Telegraph Sports Section*

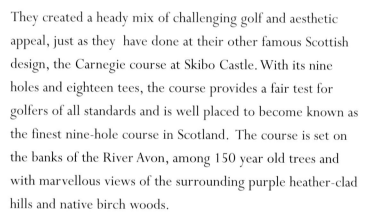

# BALLINDALLOCH'S ABERDEEN ANGUS

The Ballindalloch herd of Aberdeen Angus cattle is without doubt the oldest in the world. Black cattle have grazed peacefully in the 'Coo Haugh' beside the Castle for centuries. The beautiful race of cattle is directly descended from the native cattle found in the North East of Scotland and derives its origins from the old 'Doddies' of Angus and the 'Hummlies' from Buchan. They were all hardy, black hornless cattle whose presence in the North East of Scotland goes back to the 12th century.

*Today under the stewardship of Mrs Macpherson-Grant-Russell the black cattle still flourish in their serene setting beside the River Avon. For the last 10 years the Laird has had the honour and joy of sharing a stock Aberdeen Angus Bull with the late Queen Elizabeth the Queen Mother.*

# THE GRANTS OF BALLINDALLOCH

## 1457 - DUNCAN GRANT of Freuchie -
'Crown Tacksman of Ballindalloch'

## 1498 - JOHN GRANT
For 'Good faithful and thankful service in peace and war'. The King feus Ballindalloch and Glencairne to (Sir) Duncan Grant's grandson and successor - John Grant, 2nd Laird of Freuchie

## 1528 - JAMES GRANT, 3rd Laird of Freuchie
takes over from his father. The Ballindalloch lands are described as lying on the east bank of the Spey. Acquired the land from the Crown, no longer a Feuar. They are then bestowed on Patrick. Patrick, by marriage to one of the daughters of the Bishops of Elgin brings in the lands on the west bank of the Spey.

## LAIRDS OF BALLINDALLOCH

### PATRICK GRANT of Ballindalloch alive 1532,
Acquired lands of Ballindalloch

### JOHN GRANT of Ballindalloch
Built Ballindalloch Castle in 1546
m.(1) Isabella, dau. of John Grant of Culcabock
m.(2) Barbara Gordon

### PATRICK GRANT of Ballindalloch d.1586
m.(1) Grissel, dau of John Grant of Freuchie
m.(2) Margaret Gordon

### PATRICK GRANT of Ballindalloch gave Castle
and Estate to Brother James
m. Helen Ogilvie

### JAMES GRANT of Morinsh & Inveraven
Owned Ballindalloch

### JOHN GRANT of Ballindalloch redeemed from his
Uncle James 1633. d.c.1679
m. Elizabeth, dau. of Walter Innes of Auchintoul

### JOHN GRANT of Ballindalloch d. before 1690
m. Margaret, dau. of Sir John Leslie of Newton

### JOHN ROY GRANT of Ballindalloch
Sold estates to his cousin (c.1711)
m. Anne-Francisca, dau. of Count Patrick Leslie of Balquhain

### WILLIAM GRANT Colonel
Purchased Ballindalloch c.1711 d.1733
m. Anne Grant, dau. of Ludovick Grant of Grant

### ALEXANDER GRANT Captain
of Ballindalloch d.1751
m. Penuel, dau. of Sir James Grant of Grant

### WILLIAM GRANT Major
of Ballindalloch c.1770
m. Elizabeth, dau. of Ludovick Grant of Grangegreen,
No issue

### JAMES GRANT General
of Ballindalloch d.1806
Governor of Florida, Governor of Stirling,
NO ISSUE

### SIR GEORGE MACPHERSON-GRANT
1st Baronet of Ballindalloch, (cr. July 1838)
1781-1846 Chieftain of 'Slioch Gillies'
tribe of Macphersons
m. Mary, dau. of Thomas Carnegie of Craigo

### SIR JOHN MACPHERSON-GRANT
2nd Baronet of Ballindalloch
1804-1850 Sec. of Legation at Lisbon
m. Marion Helen, dau. of Mungo Nutter Campbell of
Ballimore, Argyll

### SIR GEORGE MACPHERSON-GRANT
3rd Baronet of Ballindalloch
1839-1907 Deputy Lieutenant counties of Banff,
Elgin and Inverness
m. Frances Elizabeth, dau. of Revd. Roger Pocklington,
Vicar of Walesby, Notts.

### SIR JOHN MACPHERSON-GRANT
4th Baronet of Ballindalloch
m. Mary Denniston
1863-1914

### SIR GEORGE MACPHERSON-GRANT
5th Baronet of Ballindalloch
1890-1950. Unmarried

### SIR EWAN GEORGE MACPHERSON-GRANT
6th and last Baronet of Ballindalloch
1907-1983.
Inherited from his cousin
m. Evelyn Nancy Stopford Dickin

### CLARE NANCY MACPHERSON-GRANT J.P
of Ballindalloch 1944-, Lord Lieutenant of Banffshire
m. Oliver Henry Russell second son of Admiral
The Hon. Sir Guy and Lady Russell

# THE WAY FORWARD

*Ask the owners of any great house and they will tell you that inheriting is the easy part; it is hanging on to the place that is hard. You have to work at it.*

*In the 1970s a new generation of Macpherson-Grants arrived at the Castle, when I brought my husband, Oliver Russell, to live in my ancestral home. The common solution to the problems associated with the upkeep of a Highland estate was to sell off land piecemeal, but the long-term folly of that approach was fully appreciated.*

*With a banking background, he realised that substantial growth in the income stream was needed to pay the salary and maintenance bills at a time when farm rents were falling behind in relative terms. Twenty-five years later there is no doubt that the strategy has worked, with the cherished family home also functioning as a successful business. Recent developments include the construction of a nine hole golf course and the leasing of land for a new wind farm.*

*What is significant is that none of this is change for its own sake. It is the sympathetic development of a Highland estate in tune with modern times: the use of innovation and forward planning to perpetuate a unique part of the heritage of a family and a nation.*

*Clan Macpherson-Grant Russell*
*Laird of Ballindalloch*

*Ballindalloch Castle*
*by Horatio McCulloch*
*1805-1867*